VIA Folios 135

Bitter Bites from Sugar Hills

Bitter Bites from Sugar Hills

Sara Fruner

BORDIGHERA PRESS

Library of Congress Control Number: 2018956515

Printed in the United States.

Published by
BORDIGHERA PRESS
John D. Calandra Italian American Institute
25 West 43rd Street, 17th Floor
New York, NY 10036

VIA FOLIOS 135
ISBN 978-1-59954-131-0

CONTENTS

to you

SPRING NOW

wearing pink air
as a balaclava
and first concocting
then humming
a crispy war cry
it is sabotaging winter
heading to outshine

criminal and terrorist
the only legitimate
green card holder
has entered the country
smuggling in a cargo
of color and wonder

EMBERS

the distance
a smile rides
to bring solace
on a broken face

the time taken
by a nod on a pact
by a head shaken
afore the frown of a fight

the patience of trains
their lilts of to and fro
love and its syrup
when a yes fools a no

consider them all
these fiery embers
as your foot lingers
on the brink of null

A MOAN

the man in the door
the guy on the floor
the girl and her mess
no tip for success

out on display
in dodgy takeaways
cappuccino flesh—
prude whispers
call it white trash

the chronicles
a street throws up
feed history—
the plump-limbed
the thick-shouldered

if you educate your ear
to the imperceptibly loud
you will hear a moan
from the gut of the earth
being chocked and torn
by a clutch on its throat

A STAIN

on your way home
after a day of scorn
missed chances
or simple jokes
you overlook
the bare foot
the dope eye
of a human being
duping her demons
in an red old top

on the pillowcase
framing your head
in your night oeuvre
a stain
is getting closer

SUBWAY SEMANTICS

the leak of beer
the lake it feeds
the feet close-by
the face beside

in rush hours
arms and legs
flood with elegies
stairways and trains
having no ideas
of all the pages
they're leaving behind
in the bustling cloud

the lingos on air
the careless looks
the horny hand
the broken film

subway semantics
overturns aesthetics
sounding like music
but chanting no ethics

HARLEM LOOP

cotton-candy hair
on sugar-cane heads
their non-stop bop
on a fairy-tale rap
this is what you meet
on 125th Street

overflowing trolleys
of good and bad
three-pointed sticks
close to limping gaits
busy with pavements
their searching
their chasing

you may think
a golden smile
is a figure of speech
here is the claim
of millennial fops
playing with teeth
instead of frocks

desire is the air
that you breathe
on 125th street
white girls' mania
digging Rasta hairdos
black men's daydream
on zeroing family weirdos

history here
is fresh and stale
you feel its gaze
blank and still
its rugged nail
getting paired
the morgue of its mouth
sealed as death
on the day of birth

RIGHTING THE WRONGS

with joy I collect
the golden laughs
some kids seed
on 72nd street

looking closer
I see red fields
spotting the cheeks
of a teenage face
standing by

her bag-pack old
her lip a bit cleft
she tucks her right foot
well behind her left

to make up
to the mocked girl
I took a paper
concrete words
built a pillory
for silliness
that lasts eternally

DOWNUNDER

there is a city
under the city
where youth dances
senility dozes—
bins eat babies
a mouth more
is trouble for sure

sad-eyed are flowers
and stink dismally
clocks pant in pain
or wait for dole
music talks politics
and theater-seats
are beds for bugs

on the skin of the city
you just spot the freckle
of a beggar begging
or a homeless roaming
you don't dig deep
you stay on the brink
and this is no wonder
dark scares any miner

with your beloved sleeping
in the room close-by
your blossoms planning
their visit in spring
you don't hear
the cry of a closed notepad
nor smell the reek of desire
left behind and gone bad

THE PURPLE HIBISCUS

a purple hibiscus
blooms on her chick-bone
no displaced tattoo
no messy foundation
but of consensus
a simple perversion

she is no child
she's tried dire straits
her breast has fed
one girl and one boy
who've grown and left

now she is alone
with her man and his ghosts
with the bible in her brains
a body of skin and bone
plus the rosary she shells

she thinks life is this
work and church
mop then lunch
bodega after friends
laundry to get done

a traveling exhibition
of rare archaeology
that is what she is
colored strata of history
written on her complexion

or maybe a murderer
killing her time
with the knickknacks
of her legacy
as a woman and partner
waiting for the very end
or the real beginning

BLACK BEAUTY

you
black beauty
a tear on your skin
a scar in your youth

your legs are praised
by profs and peers
la jeune fille
elle est une gazelle
your French teacher
is your first admirer
you are a D dreaming of a C
his moles and manners
have banned his language
from the kingdom
of your knowledge

you keep wondering
won't they see
my shaking mind
the fringe I hide it behind
the scarlet blaze
of my shame
before my father
and his jobless fame

gone girl
your wet face
is in a gum's throb
a skin's scratch
on a child's sob
your suffering
any suffering
triumphs and thrives
in places and times

Sara Fruner

I will fill ears and heads
pockets and hearts
with sacks of black confetti
notes of mute disbelief
I collect in wonder
store in faith

LOVE AFFAIR

the tang of trash
that rains squeezes
out of August dusks
meets the void
of kissless lips
of voiceless ears

this is a way to tell
about a love affair

FLASHES

I. A MENACE OF SOLACE

the moan of a glove
hosting no fingers
might comfort you
once you will see
the weight of the hand
that you have let go

II. THE DEPRESSED

in the mouth of the world
under a wounded tongue
a tooth to be pulled
waiting for its turn

SOLO DANCER

graffiti gargoyles
greet you guys
in the cave of beauty
the den of decay

molded carpets
failed quartets
bodega bags
carrying cargos
of personal mess

you are a solo dancer
shouts the madman
on the KFC corner

you must dance solo
in this city in the world
don't wait for the nod
for the green go go

no one will save you
no plastic no botox
no shrink no pill
mind the madman
his rotten bill

CITY AUSCULTATION

lying your ear
on its Cubist belly
you hear apocalypse
—or just history
and its uneven breath
if you believe history
can crawl underneath—
trains circulating
color in veins
drilling gone wild
on a new-found site

lying your eyes
on its steely bulge
you see harmless boys
and greasy pimps
bitchy ballerinas
and good old saints

in a city you can loiter
on the verge of a minute
lose your bearings
trusting the point of a finger
find your demon
perched on your neck
looking for a chat
with your cheeky self

ALL THAT GLITTERS IS NOT GOLD

bursting briefcases
of cocained brains
gun-lungs pumping
under heist-like coats
before a stupid joke
at a pharmacy clerk

armpits reeking
of bourgeois fear
when the working-class stares
at the uptown ease

sometimes it happens
you turn a clean hand
anticipating grace
and you are greeted
by five smiles of dirt
under overgrown nails

LADY LONGING

a lace of longing
on a cake of steel
is the gift
you
just-landed
get back
laying your hand
on her neck

you tiptoe dance
miles and miles
from Grand Central
to City Hall
you
unsatisfied lover
who do not dare
to enter a mall
for the fear of missing
one sigh one look
from your mistress
wiggling around you

day by day
you track runs
in her stockings
holes under armpits
her morning breath
can cook epics
of rye and chili
cold hair and sour chips
at midnight you can get
a gold piss pool
as a goodnight kiss

success can be too sweet
and mine your smile

so you go and look
for the clean mouth
of the broken souls

and there you walk
the carpet of splinters
lied down from South Ferry
all the way up
to Pelham Parkway

you can't collect every bit
of shattered dreams
can't bring home
the unspeakable face
the death of a look
the dismay on a pace

you walk side by side
your beauty and bully
the city is no liar
the city is no joker
she just does the favor
to turn her eyes
from the clock
pretending not to see
the time she wastes
playing around
with her silly devotee

Sara Fruner

AGAPE

you swallow bridges
litter and skyscrapers
you soak in sorrows
of sorrowful immigrants
and munch complaints
from moaning millennials

sometimes you think
you've had enough
now you leave the place
and look for peace
on remote shores
to detox your being
no more scrap-gobbling
enough with in-taking

the mayhem far off
you get to see
that food is no junk
that flesh is no skunk

only the deepest pitch
churns out
the purest light

THE REMEDY

to make Coney Island
drop its sad smile
I would set up a bonfire
collect paper petals
paint them with poetry
—Dante, Neruda,
Dylan of course—
sprinkle them down
the skimpy fabric
of its clown pants
and have dimples
button its cheeks

to make your tears
swim back to sea
and have your chest
be washed again
with rays of light
days of delight
I would bring your body
your pangs and distress
afore the restored cheer
on Coney Island's shore

MEN

men are no trees
a foot is no root
branches and arms
wave
to different swarms

men are no suns
well they can be at times
but just in the glow
some of them ooze
in works of art
or certain looks
like Mozart
and Louise Brooks

men are dinghies and kites
cruising seas and skies
tiny insects on some blue skin
striving for a dot to rest
and when they find it
up on air or down to earth
looking for the next

AFTER

your wrists now feel locked
your mouth ironed by a horse-bit
all the hours spent in forgetfulness
the sweet sound of eye-rubbing
the six coats of lacquer
love lays on the skin of things
the robot refrain of *no probs*
everything has collapsed
in the funnel of facts

when a dark shirt
threatens a white house
when bellies of bibles
are slit open
matter spilled over
like pork guts

you will worship schools
grow gardens
of secretive words
till lands of dissent
you will grab an arm
and drag its body
under a full moon
of a museum lamp

before is no more
indulging and soliciting
are a couple of siblings
your sanity needs eluding

today I call for a new family
living in a condo
made of Sisyphus' bricks
communicating vessels
doing stunts on a dish rack
floors woodened with haikus
and carpeted in pamphlets

THE SPOON

in the jagged horizons
piercing our noon
in the bleeding dusks
leaking on our eves
I saw portents of doom
magnificent jinxes
collecting calamities
in toddlers' giggles

I could just as well
consider the stump
on a ciggy's destiny
or a wrecked beauty
I could pick the one note
falling off-tune
in an impeccable air

but you see
no matter how iron
a spoon tastes
it still saves mouthfuls
from unnavigable seas

WOMEN WATER

the water of women
the way they have
to fill any break
to lick any crack
and fall within brackets

a sea
embracing every limb
overturning any boat
in a sky-blue roar

a cold front blowing
from up north
a draught parching
from down south
threats always covet
the liquid flesh
the milky moist

ice is not to be feared
nor toil nor sand
it is the shadow
clad in white
of a venom hand
hanging somewhere
on the original aquifer

COSMOGONY

washed away by a migraine wave
we shipwreck on a barren island
the throb of our head as festering
as the cavities in international politics

digits on forearms have not been enough
nor faces melting before toxic mushrooms
nor feet flowered on fields of fear
deadly calendars pick off endless slips

up in the air and deep down in pockets
fists are writing an eerie cosmogony where
justice can dance on the floor of fighting
and freedom survive in the hug of an armor

BODY BRAIN AND YOU

an ancient well
is the body I wear
it holds desires
weeds and corpses

a promising brain
is the future I crave
the coming and goings of hints
algorithms courting dreams

in the way you look at my wrist
while I point an empty street
or choke an innocent page
body's and brain's eyes meet

THE SNOWSTORM

prehistorical throats
of strangled engines
struggling legs
of throttled tires

not some romance
between wind and water
as written in scientists'
secret diary and fantasies

it is the white slam
of a dark hand
on the drowsy face
of the heated world

JOLT AWAKE

and the lethargy leaked in
kissing our eyes goodnight
we started dreaming
about brown minds
dancing with white heads
about flying freely
from here to there
and from there
to any somewhere

women put their knuckles
back in the dough
no pressure around
no lips dropping
a doleful *gotta go*

rifles became abstract art
on the wall of many bars
and nightsticks conducted
orchestras of stuck cars

from that lethal sleep
we've just jolt awake
with our mouth furry
from a munched trance
our eyeballs full
of reality scams

APPARENT CATASTROPHE

a battalion
of battered angels
shuffle by
their bleeding wings
their burning brains

the black body of a beetle
breaks the spell
of a white museum
as it decides to cross
its pin-neat platinum

a church grows gibbous
and the music falls
when a woman's hunch
enters the holy hall
—of nights in the cold
she smells after all

still an arch of light
flashes in your mouth
when you bow your neck
to a public tap

BATTERING AND BUTTERFLY

violet bruises
budded on bodies
scarlet daisies
landed on lips
after storms of fists

nothing of the kind
in the family you see
strolling down gaily
on 84th street

no matter
the Kandinskys
its wings display
a butterfly
is still born
a worm

THE OPPRESSED

you think they enjoy
going to the movies
getting wild at parties
cramming their woofers
their cars and attitude
with rage and sexism
not to mention solitude

the world is one thing
hard as the distance
between a nod and a no
but the truth is
the oppressed sink
in the well of themselves

sitting on this hill
my hopes dangling
on the branch of disbelief
my eyes sore
with too much watching
I spot history
dumping the past
and curling up
right here and now
its filthy boot
under a silky gown

THE CAGE

when you are born
in a hospital room
on a flight of stairs
or in a traffic hell
you always get
a pair of hands
saving your life
from your first fall

after five years or so
—yet it can be earlier
or much much later—
you see some eyes
scanning your frame
pointing your soft spot
a vine of eczema
rushing up your neck
coke-bottle glasses
cracking your charisma

when you are at school
primary or high
college or post-doc
at some point
you hear distinctly
the knife of difference
slitting your world apart

out of the bleeding cut
that you press hopeless
pours some awareness
and you slowly take in
what is going on

you have overlooked
for all those years
of blackness and whiteness

the cage of skin
that first hold
had left you in

ANATOMIES

I. SOME EYES

some eyes here
are planets
smoldering with pot
soaked of beer gloom
spinning around
in the universe of chances
bumping into broken courses

they cry and reroute
at times are total dry

dragging yourself home
you hear them rolling
behind your back
like gone games
of forlorn kids

II. SOME FACES

some faces here
are lands
cast in bronze
wrinkled rivers
stroking past
hillock cheeks

a bow takes over their head
a holler blues their mind

nonetheless
their body's aim is to impress
they hide their metro pass
CVS cards and doggie bag
behind their coolest hashtag

SONS OF INNOCENCE

a purple crest on a female skull
tattoos instead of rings
to make commitments
far more resilient
than gold and beads

a white guy in a jeans jacket
five black polished nails
the Koran resting in his lap
while he checks his emails

two girls on a wall
on Riverside Drive
sitting and kissing
their love so luminous
it could turn pitch dark
into a pool of milk

I hear tiny rifts
cracking the surfaces
of these glass existences
and I run away fast
I don't want to see
concessions nor compromises
the military muscle of nods
straightening head-shakes
and soil their purities

SONS OF EXPERIENCE

Jesus stepping down the cross
is the dude snubbing the bus
preferring to walk
his body and glam
through Marcus Garvey Park

all around he has some crack
and speed just for sale
his conscience and palms
feel soft with lack of books
a question of laziness
for sure family business

a Heineken bottle
in his father's hands
crushed his mother's teeth
a milky way of green stars
wrote his destiny
of child risen by a single mom
in an East Harlem room

brownstone has become
the hue of his future
after a white guy
has wiped away
rainbows of colors
from his juvenile sky

if inspected closer
his gait and poses
are limp and sick
however his style
in ditching the cross
while mocking mass
will bring to him
some indisputable fun
before his fated fall

CHAMELEONS AND COMEDIANS

chameleons and comedians
this people you can mock
they take streets for stages
parks for jungles of luck

you can say
they are preposterous
their work totally ridiculous
look at that one
his own poems dribbling
as coffee down a chin
and the other man
his pencil fumbling
between thumb and forefinger
missing the gist of the face
he sweats to put on paper

before poetry and art
who knows
a house full of kids
a restless mind
too shiny with wits
to sell Dunkin' Donuts

one day they had enough
or enough is what they said
they changed color
and out they went
the street the circus
their new focus

it is not the caged canary
you keep safe indoor
that carves a man
out of your matter
it is the pair of wings
you scoop out

of your dreams' coffer
and let them fly
knowing their fall
is looming close-by

BACK

a back is a book
to be read by a look
even better a stroke

with its series
of stacked disks
a spine can bind
earth and sky

evolution counts
on shoulder blades
to incubate wings
till it's time for man
to flounder ahead
to the bird he dreams

horizon of grace
when lying on a sofa
a lily of the valley
if musing over a faux pas

it is a personal diplomat
delivering a farewell note
a collective carpet
beaten by ages of torment

YOU ARE

the lighthouse
the lost call
the abracadabra
with its wall

water that kisses
a parched mouth
the flower of life
blossoming out

the golden line
my tongue
cannot etch

an amazon
her bold stretch

the rust on the waggon
moving forward
into lands of iron

light
which breeds the night
and the day
delivered with no fight

BRONX BREED

kids zooming by
cornrows sealed
with a pink teeny eye
sneakers and scooter
come second-hand
and so their father
and little brother

their heart is still
a field of green grass
and skies are countless
above their spotless skull

they do not mind
the lack of china
from their lunch tables
nor meals gasping
for healthy polyphenol
from seas of sorbitol

happiness floods their sight
every time a glass of soda
sizzles with a ray of light

NEFERTITI

the molecular structures
get rearranged
in the bodies of passers-by
and never-do-wells
when Nefertiti
steps out of past glories
out of noble agonies
to head to Clay Avenue
the sun setting
its warm hand
on her silky nape
like a tender friend

the unexpected
the syntax
arts and gods
write their epics
in the inn of heaven
or the pit of Belmont

EVERYWHERE

mirrored ties
on hipster breasts
rippled waters
of mulatto abs
rolling under
bleach blonde heads

the village is no Greenwich
it is the round-shaped room
the happy-few hang about
grooming their outfit
licking their self-esteem

if bowels fall unseen
it does not mean
rage is not scratching for vowels
perching on the puttered lip
of a chipped odd cup
or engaging the acrobat
while zipping a rope

THE ONE AND ITS OPPOSITE

what you see is wonder
framed in tourists' gapes
as much as locals' anger
caught in closing doors

within a grin
a crack
behind a step
a limp

I could dance
till night loses
its dark mood
and slips whole
into a golden coat

trees crave for running
in the skies
so viscerally
they bud leaves
colors leave bruises
and jump on kites

TELLING FIRE

just a matter of time
his teen self daydreams
head sunk in a pillow
stuffed with nightmares
mouth watering
at the luring anywheres
he'd beseech to swallow

his dad loves him dearly
and so does his wife
but it's the hand of his mom
he has pains at forgetting
as she left for a better life
after a chemio fight
at Queens Mount Sinai

cruising on a long board
the maze of woe and wonder
his neighborhood offers
he considers the library
its unspeakable depths
behind a cheap used cover
but he goes for the street
the book with skin pages
where he feels to ponder

just a matter of time
his mind writes
on his free minutes
on his school classes
you'll find the way to say
what is the crackle
you hear
every time your ear
is turned
towards the fire
parching your throat
burning your word

TIME AS A NOVEL

the instant an egg
crashes its head
on the merciless edge
of your frying pan
and there
your breakfast
is smiling back
or
the gore second
before a bubble
walks into its death
wearing pink and teal
are paragraphs
you can steal
from the time's novel
to describe what love
makes you feel

Sara Fruner

SCISSORS

bulls charge little girls
the Financial District
is not the only setting
that is witnessing

sofas serve
scissors of legs
closed tight up
then spread wide apart
and bring about
no surprise
into a bleeding heart

silence can be
the language of angels
the water sins dive in
to surface as holy souls
yet lately it is the coffin
where lost cries
and hushed noes
lay dead with no rest

at the grave side
no mourners nor grievers
just a platoon of fingers
pointing at the usual slut

SLEEPING BEAUTY

the opulent breadth
of decadent meals
saturates gaps
among edgy silences
over working lunches

someone in the subway
has spilled milk
on the platform edge
the universe might think
to stop and collect
its dropped lot
its lost path

you can walk by
bury your eyes
in your little smart pit
devote yourself
to god the unnoticed
playing online chess
or mister success
wearing headphones
looking business

when one day you look up
and find the city staring
at your shameless dozing
your senses numb
with too much null
stars gone forever
on a morning floor
you will pray
for some remedy
some new stink
to please reek by
kiss you awake
from the death bed
of your sleepy I

LOVE TRIP IN NEW YORK CITY

I. FALLING

    once I have learnt
    the language of your steps
    and grasped
    the chant of your eyes
    I took a match
    brought it closer to erudition
    and made comparisons

II. KEEP FALLING

    from your eyelids
    from your mouth
    from your navel too
    I patiently wait
    for the light
    your body
    holds captive
    and sometimes
    you fail to control
    and sometimes
    trickles into the world

III. AND FALLING

    I thought the blueberry
    was what the ink dreamt
    while the strawberry
    the transgression of creation

    I thought your word
    the ruby you offered
    in-between Dante and desire
    made of myself
    the casket you missed

IV. THE BLUE BUTTERFLY

> I used to speak in scribbles
> before sending
> the pilgrim adventurers
> of my fingertips
> to collect the artworks
> crafted by your looks
>
> the circles you walk around
> the syllables fled
> from the economics of discussions
> the red fish of ideas and occasions
> slipped away from your hold
>
> I will be the land
> storing your sheds
> seeping in your drops
> and the blue butterfly
> that from there will arise
> will be the proof
> of the sky flickering
> in our tremulous being

V. HITTING

> The exclamation mark
> your surprise planted
> when you said
> on the brink of the end
> I cannot commit
> and for this reason
> I kiss you
> for this reason
> I love you
> is still standing there
> up and high
> between farce and folly
> a bruise-blue traffic-light
> with no greens nor reds

brightening nothing
but the gorge burning
from under your steps

VI. HIGHLINE HEALING

in the solitude
my room
is arranged with
you saw bent monks
on empty bowls
endless lists
of run-out things

when I walk
up in the air
skirting the Hudson
caressing the trees
and counting the trains
which used to wink
at the shape of the bank
blood droplets
and blinding-white gauze
are but Burri and Bacon
and your hyped love
well
propaganda to pass on

SOUR AND SWEET

sour
is the taste
of skies
some days

you spot bribery
in your parlor
grease graffiti
on the bus window
your brimful head
uses as a pillow

you hear melodies sinking
in a trumpet case
when a musician—
a Motown miracle—
trades his gift
for a rent-controlled flat

you feel the rugged skin
of bygone hopes
reaching out to your clench
when you make your way
across chess-players
Krishna preachers
voodoo kings and faith healers
in one word the offspring
Union Square delivers
from Sunday to Sunday
on the bed of its stairway

when your love is too honest
the soup boiled over
and the syllables not enough
you please read the poem
a single head leaves behind
while bopping to a jiggle
or sophisticated mind

sweet
you will find
the stamp that you lick
for the next letter
you are going to send

CITY RULES

the city has plans
you would never figure
wits you will soon discover
it fools you around
by dropping a psychic
where a bar used to be
and a vet on a ring of skunk
if it feels oddly eccentric

the city feasts on blood
after killing a family diner
for a big department store
it wrapped the scene
in national tissue paper
while chocking the gore
with silver caricature

then all of a sudden
when you've fallen
from such heights
that even clouds
are afraid to tell
let alone sail
when your heart
is a shipwreck
and the world
a remote coast
the city picks you up
straightens your rags
kisses salty tracks
off of your cheeks
and sends you back
to your new old self
by bursting
just simply
into a blue noon
or a jazz thing

LAUNDRY

on Amsterdam Avenue
between 140th and 141st
where bricks are the law
and men are often found
carrying boom-box cases
which burst with comfort music
and probably some old poltergeist
you step into a fragrant mist

you think
you must be mistaken
there is no laundress
no stone fountain
no Gervaise scrubbing away
Francophone greasiness
yet you are pretty sure
that's smell of clean
that's soap regime

forget about
machines and dryers
five-dollar bills
to reload cash cards
a laundry in a basement
can rule a corner
can make your day
it is scent stopping stink
literature washing away
a sidewalk and its dirt

SPIRITUALITY

seven days a week
pavements are porns
on Broadway and Bleecker
on Madison and Fifth
where multi-ethnic carnage
is the street-written script

on Sundays
the city temple
opens its gates
to sports devotees
craving for punishment
and to heartbroken flock
begging friends and folk
for absolution and atonement

here spirituality
has nothing to do
with Hail Marys
and God forbids
it washes to your shore
other's transgressions
hoping you come out
with a brand-new bible
written by your hand
page after page
every passing day

THE HOLE IN THE UNIVERSE

the prodigy we were
in the middle of the night
our glow was visible
from Sinatra Drive
up to Hamilton Heights

the brightness that shined
when an intuition
flashed through your mind
the fluorescent words
I squeezed from language
to mimic the effect
on my little notepad

then one day
a line cracked
on a baby cheek
a boat on the Lake
amid Central Park
coveted wreckage
and the two thousands
twenty-seven bridges
stapling land to water
on the nation of the natives
pulled like stitches
on a fresh-slain finger

as big as New York is
from Wakefield
down to Bay Ridge
it was not enough
to hold and encompass
the glorious apocalypse
of us without us

it will take ages
for people to realize

the rayless sun they see
in full moon nights
is the hole love etched
to escape the universe

THE SAD SONG OF THE SOCIAL LONER

if you are quiet at night
committed to fight back
a full list of noises
including
throat-clearing works
shriek-drilling jungles
of digital greenness
bills clamoring justice
in any single business
hopes opposing fear
in non-for-profit offices

if you summon silence
as a court witness
just for few minutes
you will be touched
by a strange sad song
which is not so sad
but you know
music is the hand
that leads your soul
to the brink of tears
after all

this city is no city
of gods and gurus—
divas and kings
reign in other counties
mainly Californian
of course in the Vatican

this is the city
of social loners
speaking to mirrors
searching for shelter
in staggering jobs

rooms drenched in shade
and same old helter skelter

they swarm an island
of danger and marvel
with alarm and faith
their juvenile wings
regularly assaulted
by the down-to-earth

BLANK IS THE COLOR OF LOST MEMORY

history reeks and throbs
its skin is covered
in sores and boils
since when the apeman
killed bunnies and bucks
to shut up his growling guts

a demolition ball
to level uneven grounds
and clear out thorny yards
is called Soweto
the fabrication of a space
to lodge uneasy waste
turning unwelcome subjects
into welcome outcasts
be they of flesh or iron
marble or cotto
is called a ghetto

blank is the color
of lost memory
only by having
troubles and unease
plague and disease
shining red and rot
on your daily track
there is a chance
for your face
to use a grimace
for a question mark
to fire the murk
of single thought

DEDUCTION

if you believe
pouring plastic
into a wrinkle
will fight age
shut the bird of beauty
into a safe cage
you will most likely
feel at ease
roaming around
an empty archive
or nod in assent
at pages of history
written in white

AMNESIA

my body swimming
belly blinking
at the sea floor
back flirting
with the sky above
in a matter of seconds
a pig-shaped shade
groped the girly light

just a cloud passing by
I thought jovially
or some prehistoric bird
making fun of the sun

back on the beach
my moves stopped
my mouth dropped
the feeling of skin
getting snagged
amid itch and stretch

no matter the amnesia
you can buy for cheap
you'll never get away
from the day you live

DREAM COME TRUE

far away from the center
there was a special field
where statues and plaques
could live in peace

after cast iron lost its grip
and horses managed to flee
squares had grown into shrines
for a bench and a tree

people seemed unaffected
a smile in the right place
the daily clock dictating
this plan and that pace

yet they staggered a bit
their limbs uncoordinated
looking a little stoned
somewhat offbeat

their flats stored no books
but stacks and flocks
of flying notes
worshipping old hat

gasping awake
I was clinging
on a scrap of paper
my hand bleeding

THE BARBARIANS

resting your head
in the nook of your hopes
or of someone's hug
you lower your drawbridge
open up to who-knows

if they happen to be
the Barbarians
there is nothing
you can really do

just wait for their hoard
to raise dramatic palaces
and tear them down
sniff up any chemical
to be found and seen
and then veer to straight edge
hand raised for tox screen

in case you wonder
who's the first of the list
one worthy of Attila
Alaric and Theodoric
well
love
no need to tell

they can also be
fathers
friends and gods
of films or fashion
any of that sort

if you push them back
chances are
you will be designated

Eden the Second
known as The Wretched
the prettiest garden
with utmost luxury
withered to death
for lack of agony

PORNOGRAPHY

the coils of sirens
swirling in the air
the philosophy of lunatics
unfolding in the subway
you can label it all
day-to-day administration
but as a matter of fact
it is the city's doing
its cunning orchestration

despite looking on its own
free from want and need
it can't stay away from you
it creeps under your windows
regardless of sash menaces
it chases you in libraries
churches and funerals
it even joins in festivities
family awkward silences

some people say bye
get a one-way ticket
to stop feeling its breadth
down their battered neck
seven days a week
they cast curses
pour out disgraces
on a number of things
like that goddam wind
those insane rents

don't know exactly
if you ever recover
from the condition
of seeing beauty and horror
making love in the open
every hour every corner

that kind of pornography
calls for monastic resilience
not to mention
a knack for masochism

FATHER

we share papers
but our countries differ
you used to speak silence
when my lungs swole in joy
or shrank in sorrow
no amount of terror
could bring your legs
to reach my arms

you were a Gothic tower
and a moat all around
I stood on dry land
trying all the time
to find the way
to cross that water

I would have accepted
any means any lift
even Charon's
I would have held
his blazing gaze
with no Virgil
at my side

wrath is among the bestsellers
on the nightstand of teenagers
as a girl I devoured it too
and spat its fiery flowers
every time I could

no transition was ever possible
no translation either
your dictionary came out
in one single copy
for just one owner
my dictionary
is still a bolgia of scraps

expecting a philologist
or maybe a good lover
to organize them all
from cover to cover

now that I am here
watching hell and paradise
on this island of brittle souls
seeking to steady their grounds
I see how baby your being was
under your shaggy old skin
you could have never survived
the blasphemous aesthetics
behind my razor grammar
before my madcap outfits

forgetfulness
is food for gods
and words are too
so I sit on the sill
of this white window
and plan a house
with means I get
bricks I collect
and stare outside
anticipating works

MERCY

brothers checking sisters
while collecting mail
in the Marcy Houses
as bad things happen
to girls in a stair

a Latino lifting a trunk
for a senior Latino
on the avenue named
after Adam Powell
where indifference
can be an act of power

picking the rotten tooth
within a beaming smile
is the daily agenda
of haters of any kind
New York City's
point out brass towers
ivy league scavengers
all the sparkling junk
smelling of shiny want

apart from the caring bro
and the helpful Latino
they fail to report
a tiny little lighthouse
glowing-eyed and flamy
working as warner
a scarlet-clad angel
that guards the river
and whispers in fable

THE BAG

the bag where I collect
all sort of unsorted waste
is the gift I got
when I came to light

the city mothers
progenies of ruins
wonderful treasures
of damaged souls
luminous holes
that crushed hopes
navigate across

all the mistakes
a woman makes
for too much love
too much care
too much crave

the mangy velvet
of a violin case
touched by clemency
in the shape of money

the cherry pit
a lover sucks
anticipating
garnet flesh
shaped as lips

forbidden food
scampered out
of Nazi diets
taxi leather seats
untold affairs
glide onto
from door to door

poets belong
to the category
of junk dealers
but considering
past is their matter
they never part
from the jumble
they assemble

wretched as it sounds
they carry everything
and sell nothing
they trust the place
will be searched through
by some curious face

CHISELS AND STONE

after ten pm
when dark is lace
sewn around everyone
and the city is wide awake
it's likely some acumen
descends from up above
or surfaces from down under

daylight is enemy
of things revealed
its radiant program
is the best cloak
secrecy can sink in

night is the voice of truth
not anyone is willing to hear
that's why sleep is so popular
that's why falling in its net
pushed by chemistry or by nature
for at least seven unbroken hours
is inscribed in the tablets of culture

we are lucky souls
every artist's home
and not just the sculptor's
is a mess of chisels and stone

END

the day you left
after the boxes drama
the hammock can stay
the walls weeping away
the paintings we bought

the day of a life dying
a new one yet unborn
and you and me in-between
trying to make fun
of the blender I broke
by grinding dry bread

that very day
the moon turned its back
and after some initial unrest
the earth adjusted to dark

I WISH I COULD

sense the serious moments in life
grant gold to golden occasions
cry rivers when rivers need a cry
stretch-to-burst the border of decency
bomb the line between concern and apathy
abstain from diving into the pool of honesty
when its water can burn too tender a body
confess that deserts still scorch my tongue
every time I say his name out loud

Sara Fruner

REQUIEM FOR THE THINGS NOT DONE

the lives never lived
the men never loved
the books to be read
that lie on the shelf

I am sure there's a dome
hosting the full list
of what's untried and gone
a sacred place
packed with wishes
from floor to steeples
let me give two examples

walking on 14th Street
wearing nothing more
than sequins of desire
a turban of silk insight

being in a museum at night
listening to the silence crack
under the passing of time
over the skin of a portrait

STILL LIFE

the air swims in
on River Terrace
slivers of peach light
are the sweet of the day
served on the floor
by the evening sky

the Jersey lurches
on the edge over there
invoking the push
that will make it land
on the bandwagon
right here

somewhere close
a coarse hand crumples
the sheet of democracy
you hear the screech
of words and hopes
being crushed
and hushed

the future could house
promise and sparkles
hours of knowledge
after days of finding
instead it will array
rows of tired heads
bent on setting right
everything crooked
and mending rips

YESTERDAY

a pair of muddy boots
butchered a path of lilacs
a pool of violet blood
bloomed into the pad
and soaked in fast

dark will be the buds
blossoming next spring
and they will rot
before building up
into beds of flowers
believe it or not

SHADOW

a marriage over
months in a fleapit
some lousy job
you cannot quit

deception is the bread
baked and gobbled
every day
to get by

honesty pays peanuts
and demands the world
if you try to taste it
milk and honeydew
are not to be got
quite the opposite
you will scowl
at another go

if your answer is no
and your life feels just fine
keep considering your shadow
a photography phenomenon

Sara Fruner

HYMN TO THE VANISHED WORLD

you had it all
the lands the oceans messed up
and then put them back
to shove in meaning and progress
the success god claimed on himself

you had the sun
that you melt in glass
the voice
in minutes of peace
and sex under seas of silk

you had the core of the matter
fluttering with its stingy beat
the soul stowed in living paintings
footnotes below revolutionary theories

you had watermelons
to replicate smiles
delights of tobacco and wine
to slam Eden's gates wide

you had wheels
to defeat distances
forks and plates
to rescue pulp
from abysmal diets

you had seismographs
plasters and junkyards
the way to spawn
phosphines in your sight

you had hair and canopies
from which minds and veggies
squeezed out theorems
from winters to summers

you had light
flowing in your veins
when accidental encounters
would raise domes of glee
around you two faithful
and you two grateful
would fall on your knees
under alcoholic whispers
of erotic liturgies

you had air
you could write
in waves and rhythm
laughter and pipers

you had pens full of books
portable screens
lines of flat bellies
pregnant with Word promises

you had daffodils
the rings of gold they set free
if wind would toss them loose
you had rattles
the rings of silver shut in exile
if they laid untouched longtime

you had the way to feel
as a disaster averted
or a dish just cleaned

you had the fury of poets
in the painters' fingers
the genius' libido
picking up satyrs' lilies
from pure mathematics

we had all this
in that time
of comforts and narcosis

now
slow and fat
unable of hubris
we beg for light
within a blind orbit

ARTISTIC STATEMENT

In November 2016, I moved to Sugar Hill, Harlem, after a decade of longing for New York City—my geographical soulmate.

Provided with a cityscape that somehow welcomed, with all its contradictions, the poetic self, I started cruising the streets, searching people's eyes, listening to the endless epics the city narrates every day, every night. New York is a storyteller nobody can silence. My recording of its voice comes from a pure act of love towards the extraordinary repository of diverse humanity the city proves to be. Beauty here can sparkle with horror, disgust and trauma, and still be utterly gracious. This contrast, in its fierce vividness, has opened up a new territory that my imagination never gets tired of exploring.

I also began questioning the political moment in which I landed here, with the world stepping into some new global Middle Ages, and faltering on major long-standing issues—including discrimination, violence on women, race disparities—and on history itself.

If my poetry in Italian primarily focuses on an intimate pursuit, where the universal might resonate in the poetic subject's individual experience, *Bitter Bites from Sugar Hills* addresses the current world we are living.

My poetic imagery moves around archetypal recurring images, which could suggest some poietic consistency, but which I am more prone to define deep-rooted obsessions: pain, wonder, desire, solitude, mourning, loss, god, the quest for beauty in an ethically and environmentally lacerated world. And love, of course.

ON POETRY,
AND ON WRITING IN ENGLISH
AS AN ITALIAN

To me, poetry means searching the unknown. Trying to delve into it, catch it, make some sense out of it, then articulate it through language, and share it. Even at the risk of my poetry falling ununderstood, or being felt as obscure—art, after all, holds a secret side, which you will never grasp, which will always remain unfathomable.

I am not interested in what is given, or in chanting the patent beauty of breath-taking views. What is already there, and visible, can be left to fiction, or non-fiction—or the phone-directory, for that matter.

The tiniest and the gigantic, the doleful and the down-and-out. The broken, the beaten and the bruised. All these, and many others, are the beloved subjects of my quest as a poet.

People tend to find writing in a language other than one's own quite peculiar, even more so if the chosen genre is poetry. For me, it is a free choice, which encapsulates philosophy, politics and pleasure. English allows me to investigate unexplored emotional and intellectual areas while being surrounded by a specific geo-linguistic context. With politics leaking into poetics, my tongue has slipped into another language and has become a blade, which feels likewise committed to carve beauty out of the dull matter of the everyday.

At the same time, English fills my mouth with unprecedented sweetness. English is the candy language my tongue has always enjoyed savoring. This does not mean Italian is bitter. Italy can be. Italian won't ever.

ABOUT THE AUTHOR

Sara Fruner was born in Riva del Garda, Trentino. After graduating in English literature and language at Ca' Foscari University (Venice), and specializing in literary translation from the English at Istituto Superiore Interpreti e Traduttori, Fondazione Scuole Civiche Milano, and at Ca' Foscari, she has been working as a translator in the publishing industry, mainly for Giunti Editore. Being interested in post-colonial literature, her translations include works by Dionne Brand, Monique Truong, Sello Duiker, Raj Rao and Don McKay.

After serving at the Italian Cultural Institute of Los Angeles in 2007, she has worked for six years as Senior Publication Coordinator in an international research center based in Trento, and taught English as a foreign language at Istituto Accademico per Interpreti e Traduttori di Trento (ISIT).

In 2016, she moved to New York City, where she currently teaches Italian at the Fashion Institute of Technology and at Mercy College, contributes to newsmagazine *La Voce di New York,* and collaborates as interpreter/performer at the Center for Italian Modern Art.

The place between English and Italian is what she calls "home." Swinging there, while writing poetry, her favorite activity.

VIA FOLIOS

A refereed book series dedicated to the culture of Italians and Italian Americans.

KATHY CURTO. *Not for Nothing*, Vol. 134. Essays. $16

JENNIFER MARTELLI. *My Tarantella*. Vol. 133. Poetry. $10

MARIA TERRONE. *At Home in the New World*. Vol. 132. Essays. $16

GIL FAGIANI. *Missing Madonnas*. Vol. 131. Poetry. $14

LEWIS TURCO. *The Sonnetarium*. Vol. 130. Poetry. $12

JOE AMATO. *Samuel Taylor's Hollywood Adventure*. Vol. 129. Novel. $20

BEA TUSIANI. *Con Amore*. Vol. 128. Memoir. $16

MARIA GIURA. *What My Father Taught Me*. Vol. 127. Poetry. $12

STANISLAO PUGLIESE. *A Century of Sinatra*. Vol. 126. Popular Culture. $12

TONY ARDIZZONE. *The Arab's Ox*. Vol. 125. Novel. $18

PHYLLIS CAPELLO. *Packs Small Plays Big*. Vol. 124. Literature.

FRED GARDAPHÉ. *Read 'em and Reap*. Vol. 123. Criticism. $22

JOSEPH A. AMATO. *Diagnostics*. Vol 122. Literature. $12.

DENNIS BARONE. *Second Thoughts*. Vol 121. Poetry. $10

OLIVIA K. CERRONE. *The Hunger Saint*. Vol 120. Novella. $12

GARIBLADI M. LAPOLLA. *Miss Rollins in Love*. Vol 119. Novel. $24

JOSEPH TUSIANI. *A Clarion Call*. Vol 118. Poetry. $16

JOSEPH A. AMATO. *My Three Sicilies*. Vol 117. Poetry & Prose. $17

MARGHERITA COSTA. *Voice of a Virtuosa and Coutesan*. Vol 116. Poetry. $24

NICOLE SANTALUCIA. *Because I Did Not Die*. Vol 115. Poetry. $12

MARK CIABATTARI. *Preludes to History*. Vol 114. Poetry. $12

HELEN BAROLINI. *Visits*. Vol 113. Novel. $22

ERNESTO LIVORNI. *The Fathers' America*. Vol 112. Poetry. $14

MARIO B. MIGNONE. *The Story of My People*. Vol 111. Non-fiction. $17

GEORGE GUIDA. *The Sleeping Gulf*. Vol 110. Poetry. $14

JOEY NICOLETTI. *Reverse Graffiti*. Vol 109. Poetry. $14

GIOSE RIMANELLI. *Il mestiere del furbo*. Vol 108. Criticism. $20

LEWIS TURCO. *The Hero Enkidu*. Vol 107. Poetry. $14

AL TACCONELLI. *Perhaps Fly*. Vol 106. Poetry. $14

RACHEL GUIDO DEVRIES. *A Woman Unknown in Her Bones*. Vol 105. Poetry. $11

BERNARD BRUNO. *A Tear and a Tear in My Heart*. Vol 104. Non-fiction. $20

FELIX STEFANILE. *Songs of the Sparrow*. Vol 103. Poetry. $30

FRANK POLIZZI. *A New Life with Bianca*. Vol 102. Poetry. $10

GIL FAGIANI. *Stone Walls*. Vol 101. Poetry. $14

LOUISE DESALVO. *Casting Off*. Vol 100. Fiction. $22

MARY JO BONA. *I Stop Waiting for You*. Vol 99. Poetry. $12

RACHEL GUIDO DEVRIES. *Stati zitt, Josie*. Vol 98. Children's Literature. $8

GRACE CAVALIERI. *The Mandate of Heaven*. Vol 97. Poetry. $14

MARISA FRASCA. *Via incanto*. Vol 96. Poetry. $12

DOUGLAS GLADSTONE. *Carving a Niche for Himself*. Vol 95. History. $12

MARIA TERRONE. *Eye to Eye*. Vol 94. Poetry. $14

CONSTANCE SANCETTA. *Here in Cerchio*. Vol 93. Local History. $15

MARIA MAZZIOTTI GILLAN. *Ancestors' Song*. Vol 92. Poetry. $14

MICHAEL PARENTI. *Waiting for Yesterday: Pages from a Street Kid's Life*. Vol 90. Memoir. $15

ANNIE LANZILLOTTO. *Schistsong*. Vol 89. Poetry. $15

EMANUEL DI PASQUALE. *Love Lines*. Vol 88. Poetry. $10

CAROSONE & LOGIUDICE. *Our Naked Lives*. Vol 87. Essays. $15

JAMES PERICONI. *Strangers in a Strange Land: A Survey of Italian-Language American Books*.Vol 86. Book History. $24

DANIELA GIOSEFFI. *Escaping La Vita Della Cucina*. Vol 85. Essays. $22

MARIA FAMÀ. *Mystics in the Family*. Vol 84. Poetry. $10

ROSSANA DEL ZIO. *From Bread and Tomatoes to Zuppa di Pesce "Ciambotto"*.Vol. 83. $15

LORENZO DELBOCA. *Polentoni*. Vol 82. Italian Studies. $15

SAMUEL GHELLI. *A Reference Grammar*. Vol 81. Italian Language. $36

ROSS TALARICO. *Sled Run*. Vol 80. Fiction. $15

FRED MISURELLA. *Only Sons*. Vol 79. Fiction. $14

FRANK LENTRICCHIA. *The Portable Lentricchia*. Vol 78. Fiction. $16

RICHARD VETERE. *The Other Colors in a Snow Storm*. Vol 77. Poetry. $10

GARIBALDI LAPOLLA. *Fire in the Flesh*. Vol 76 Fiction & Criticism. $25

GEORGE GUIDA. *The Pope Stories*. Vol 75 Prose. $15

ROBERT VISCUSI. *Ellis Island*. Vol 74. Poetry. $28

ELENA GIANINI BELOTTI. *The Bitter Taste of Strangers Bread*. Vol 73. Fiction. $24

PINO APRILE. *Terroni*. Vol 72. Italian Studies. $20

EMANUEL DI PASQUALE. *Harvest*. Vol 71. Poetry. $10

ROBERT ZWEIG. *Return to Naples*. Vol 70. Memoir. $16

AIROS & CAPPELLI. *Guido*. Vol 69. Italian/American Studies. $12

FRED GARDAPHÉ. *Moustache Pete is Dead! Long Live Moustache Pete!*. Vol 67. Literature/Oral History. $12

PAOLO RUFFILLI. *Dark Room/Camera oscura*. Vol 66. Poetry. $11

HELEN BAROLINI. *Crossing the Alps*. Vol 65. Fiction. $14

COSMO FERRARA. *Profiles of Italian Americans*. Vol 64. Italian Americana. $16

GIL FAGIANI. *Chianti in Connecticut*. Vol 63. Poetry. $10

BASSETTI & D'ACQUINO. *Italic Lessons*. Vol 62. Italian/American Studies. $10

CAVALIERI & PASCARELLI, Eds. *The Poet's Cookbook*. Vol 61. Poetry/Recipes. $12

EMANUEL DI PASQUALE. *Siciliana*. Vol 60. Poetry. $8

NATALIA COSTA, Ed. *Bufalini*. Vol 59. Poetry. $18.

RICHARD VETERE. *Baroque*. Vol 58. Fiction. $18.

LEWIS TURCO. *La Famiglia/The Family*. Vol 57. Memoir. $15

NICK JAMES MILETI. *The Unscrupulous*. Vol 56. Humanities. $20

BASSETTI. ACCOLLA. D'AQUINO. *Italici: An Encounter with Piero Bassetti*. Vol 55. Italian Studies. $8

GIOSE RIMANELLI. *The Three-legged One*. Vol 54. Fiction. $15

LEWIS TURCO. *Shaking the Family Tree*. Vol 15. Memoirs. $9

LUIGI RUSTICHELLI, Ed. *Seminario sulla drammaturgia*. Vol 14. Theater/ Essays. $10

FRED GARDAPHÈ. *Moustache Pete is Dead! Long Live Moustache Pete!*. Vol 13. Oral Literature. $10

JONE GAILLARD CORSI. *Il libretto d'autore. 1860 – 1930*. Vol 12. Criticism. $17

HELEN BAROLINI. *Chiaroscuro: Essays of Identity*. Vol 11. Essays. $15

PICARAZZI & FEINSTEIN, Eds. *An African Harlequin in Milan*. Vol 10. Theater/Essays. $15

JOSEPH RICAPITO. *Florentine Streets & Other Poems*. Vol 9. Poetry. $9

FRED MISURELLA. *Short Time*. Vol 8. Novella. $7

NED CONDINI. *Quartettsatz*. Vol 7. Poetry. $7

ANTHONY JULIAN TAMBURRI, Ed. *Fuori: Essays by Italian/American Lesbiansand Gays*. Vol 6. Essays. $10

ANTONIO GRAMSCI. P. Verdicchio. Trans. & Intro. *The Southern Question*. Vol 5.Social Criticism. $5

DANIELA GIOSEFFI. *Word Wounds & Water Flowers*. Vol 4. Poetry. $8

WILEY FEINSTEIN. *Humility's Deceit: Calvino Reading Ariosto Reading Calvino*. Vol 3. Criticism. $10

PAOLO A. GIORDANO, Ed. *Joseph Tusiani: Poet. Translator. Humanist*. Vol 2. Criticism. $25

ROBERT VISCUSI. *Oration Upon the Most Recent Death of Christopher Columbus*. Vol 1. Poetry.